POEMS From HESED

Selections From Collections

As Received by Barbara Knowles

iUniverse, Inc.
New York   Bloomington

POEMS From HESED
Selections From Collections

Cover "In The Beginning GOD...." Designed by Diana Setiawan

All Scripture Is Quoted Or Inspired by The King James Version Of The BIBLE

iUniverse books may be ordered through booksellers or by contacting:

iUniverse
1663 Liberty Drive
Bloomington, IN 47403
www.iuniverse.com
1-800-Authors (1-800-288-4677)

ISBN: 978-1-4502-3956-1 (sc)
ISBN: 978-1-4502-3958-5 (ebook)

Library of Congress Control Number: 2010909468

Printed in the United States of America

iUniverse rev. date: 08/20/2010

THANKS BE UNTO~

Those To Whom Much Appreciation Is Due.

Down The Hall She Was Prayin' For Me
Naomi ie..... A Bulldog In GOD'S ARMY
Such HOLY GHOST TENACITY!!
She Among Others In GOD'S INFANTRY
HIS RESCUE TEAM~ For Whom No Mission
Was Too Mean!! Maria Who Wrote Poetry~
Doris Too~ Always Looking Unto....
The Author And Finisher Of The FAITH ie.
JESUS THE CHRIST~ YESHUA HA YEHUDI.
Then Vera And Maria #2 With Whom
I Was With In The Land Of The Jew...
Not To Forget My Family~ Bill My Brother~
Into Poetry Before Me~Jane With Her Gift
For Photography And Sid With Her Visits Lightened
The Load And Friends In ISRAEL With Whom
Time I Did Spend; Sarah~ Sonia~ Ragna ~Shlomit
Ellen~ Miriam And Ruthie Too~ From Their
Lives GOD Contributed Too And Marshall Beeber
With His Website Hosted For Me So Many Pieces
Of Poetry. To You All I Give Thanks And Render
GOD Praise....

For All Of Your Love And Prayers
In These Last Days.
As I Come To Know HIM~ JESUS The CHRIST My
SAVIOUR My Kin.. Grafted In To HIS FAMILY
A Miracle Come To Be.~ Now Followed By This
Book Of Poetry. Because Of HIS GRACE Extended
To Me The Pen-Name Is Chosen~ HESED ie.

HESED-Heb. GOD'S GRACE & MERCY

A GIFT OF WORDS

GOD Has Given Me
HIS Gift Of Words
Thereby Men's Souls
Will Be Stirred.

HESED

GOD Gave Dictation
HE Later Gave
Confirmation~
Helped Me To Find
That Which Was Written
Was From HIS MIND.

HESED
Philippians 2:5

INTRODUCTION

These Poems Are Selected From Seventeen Collections Which
Came As "Dictation" From Heaven.How Could This Be??!!
GOD HIMSELF Extended HIS GRACE AND MERCY Unmerited
Favor~HIS HESED (Chesed- Hebrew) To Me.
From BORN AGAIN Unto The End The Poems Vary In
"Genre." Having Lived In Israel Over A Period Of Six Years
A Growing Awareness Came~ GOD sent HIS SON A Jew.
That HIS LOVE IS Still Is Extended To Them Too. So Many
Poems Therefore Include "JESUS THE JEW" GOD'S PLAN
For Them To Return To THE LAND. HE Has THE PLAN.
See Poems On Israel And America~ Our Important Role
To Cooperate Lest We Continue To Get "Retaliates"
Reproofs ie. For Not Considering That When We Push
Israel Against GOD'S PLAN We Put America In Jeopardy.
The Whole World Is Part Of This LAST DAYS "Stage."
GOD Is Not Willing That Any Should Perish But That We
Would Come HIM To Cherish.
For Years I Had Read The Old Testament Over And Was
Very Sure Of GOD'S PLAN For The JEW~ Then It Became
Evident HE Was Showing That There Were Sins In Me Too
Are You Outside Of All??!! GOD Said..

The Poems Continued To Come~ Recalling Verses From
The Old And New Testaments~ The Bible Comprehensive ie.
May It All Be A Blessing To You In The Name Of JESUS The
CHRIST ~YESHUA The JEW.

HESED
As Received by Barbara Knowles June 4, 2010

*In The Beginning Was The Word, And The Word Was With GOD,
And THE WORD Was GOD... John 1:1*

TABLE OF CONTENTS

SHORTS

BALLADS

HOLY DAYS ~ HOLIDAYS

OTHERS AFTER PASSOVER

ADD~ONS

BORN AGAIN

BORN AGAIN

Born Again
Saved from Sin.
Blood on the Altar
Do not Falter.
Come to HIM Now.
Bow ~ Bow ~ Bow!
For HE is LORD.
The LIVING WORD.
Of WHOM Prophets Spoke.
In Whom You can HOPE
For Life Eternal
Joys Supernal
Living Water
Do Not Falter.
HE is THE ONE
JESUS GOD'S SON.

HESED
Leviticus 17:11
John 3:3 & 5 & 7 & 16-17

I Read A Very "Graphic"! Book On Hell
GOD Woke Me UP In The Middle
Of The Night~ Giving Me This Poem.
Born Again ~ GOD'S ANTIDOTE For Sin

AT-ONE-MEANT

Meant To Be
At ONE With GOD
Only Possible Through
The Shed Blood
Of HIS SON
Not ThroughThe "Works"
We Have Done
YESHUA~JESUS
Looks For Faith In Us~
That We Look To HIM!
Then All Things
Are Possible HE Said It~
Never "Dread" It!
That Which Is A
"Block" In Your Life~
Speak To That Mountain~
And You Will SEE
Your FAITH Grow
From A Seed To A TREE.

HESED
Matthew 17:20 & Ephesians 2:8-9
Hebrews 11:6

STILL ? STILL STILL !

I Will "Fix" You -
And You Will See.
When You Come To ME.
All The Others To
Whom You Have Been -
They Have Not Solved
Your Problem Of
Sin And Self-Will.
Still? I Love You
Still. BE STILL!
LOOK TO JESUS
HE Loves You STILL.

HESED

THE DIVINE ALTERNATIVE

The Divine Alternative
Take It!!
Thereby You Can
Paint The Sky.

GOD Has Prepared It
For You
Through HIS SON
JESUS THE JEW.

HESED
Psalm 103:11-18

Behind These Poems There is a Thought.
With a Price -We are Bought.
1 Corinthians 6:20

"PAINT THE SKY"~ Title Of Another Collection

HUMBLE YOURSELF

The More You are HUMBLE
The Less You Will STUMBLE!
HUMBLE YOURSELF.
COME UNTO HIM.
Confess The Sin.
HE is ABLE
To Make You STABLE.

HESED
Psalm 32:5 & Matthew 23:12
1 Peter 5:6

EVERYTHING THAT...

Can Be Shaken....
Look At The Shaking!!
She's Going Through ~
She's Going THROUGH!!
It Has To Do With YOU.
YOU Who Are LORD
Fulfilling YOUR WORD
That When THE Shaking Comes
We Are Not Stirred~
Standing On YOUR WORD.

HESED
Hebrews 12:27

So Many "Things" Happening At Once!
But GOD!!

ETERNAL REST

Entering In To
Eternal Rest
This Is GOD'S BEST.
The Question Is HOW???
The Route Has Been Given
By Way Of MESSIAH ~
All Leaven Is "Ridden"
Sin Forgiven ~
YOM KIPPUR
For The Jew And
All Mankind
YESHUA~ JESUS
HE Is The DOOR.

HESED
Psalm 116:15

BUT GOD WILL REDEEM..

PSALM 49:15
But God Will Redeem My Soul From The Power Of The
Grave For He Shall Receive Me. Selah.

PSALM 66:18-20
If I Regard Iniquity In My Heart, The Lord Will Not Hear Me:
But Verily God Hath Heard Me; He Hath Attended To The
Voice Of My Prayer. Blessed Be God, Which Hath Not Turned
Away My Prayer, Nor His Mercy From Me.

PSALM 73:24
Thou Shalt Guide Me With Thy Counsel, And Afterward
Receive Me To Glory.

HEBREWS 2:14-15
[14]Forasmuch Then As The Children Are Partakers Of Flesh
And Blood, He Also Himself Likewise Took Part Of The Same;
That Through Death He Might Destroy Him That Had The
Power Of Death, That Is, The Devil;
[15]And Deliver Them Who Through Fear Of Death Were All
Their Lifetime Subject To Bondage.

JOB 19:25
For I Know That My Redeemer Liveth, And That He Shall
Stand At The Latter Day Upon The Earth:

TO WHOM GOD WOULD MAKE KNOWN..

COLOSSIANS 1:27

27To Whom God Would Make Known What Is The Riches Of The Glory Of This Mystery Among The Gentiles; Which Is Christ In You, The Hope Of Glory:

1 JOHN 5:11-13

11And This Is The Record, That God Hath Given To Us Eternal Life, And This Life Is In His Son.
12He That Hath The Son Hath Life; And He That Hath Not The Son Of God Hath Not Life.
13These Things Have I Written Unto You That Believe On The Name Of The Son Of God; That Ye May Know That Ye Have Eternal Life, And That Ye May Believe On The Name Of The Son Of God.

GOD'S ENDEAVOR

Philippians 4:13

HE IS THE LIGHT

Some Day I Pray That
LIGHT Will Shine Through
The LIGHT That Is
From JESUS THE JEW.
HE IS LIGHT.
LIGHT To The Soul.
HE Gives That Sight
To Make One Whole.
Whole In The Body
Whole In The Soul.
Given By HIM
That Is HIS ROLE~
Wholeness In Your Spirit Too
From JESUS The JEW.

HESED
John 12:46

And GOD Said, Let There Be Light And There Was Light.. Genesis 1:3

NOT DETERRED

Born To Be Servants.
GOD Is MOVING
"DETERRENTS!!"
Out Of HIS And Our Way
IF We Just Pray~
In THIS LAST DAY!!!.
HE Is Hastening
HIS WORD TO PERFORM IT.
It Is Therefore Important
That We Sit And Spend
Time With HIM And
HIS WORD~ Thereby
We Are Not D E TE R R E D!!

HESED
Jeremiah 1:12

"LENGTHEN"

To Be Strengthened
You Must "Lengthen"
The Cords Of Your Tent..
Not To Remain Where You Are
Under That "Strain"
Wherein You Are Weak~
But "Lengthen" And
JESUS Will Strengthen
As HIM You Seek.
"LAUNCH OUT Into
The DEEP" ~ Even
This Week!

HESED
Isaiah 54:2 & Luke 5:4

ROMANS 8:28

This Could Be
A Devastating
Set Back!!"
Or Could It Be
GOD'S Way Of
Getting On The
Right "Track!!"
HE Is Never Late
Remember
ROMANS EIGHT
And That Verse
Twenty Eight!!

HESED
*"And We KNOW That ALL Things Work
Together For Good To Them That Love GOD
To Them Who Are The Called According To HIS
"Purpose." ~ Romans 8:28.*

GOD Gave Me This Prior To 911 ! ! !

SAMARIA

As JESUS Had To Go Through
S A M A R I A
Is There Some Area Where
You Have Not Let HIM In??
JESUS THE CHRIST
Who Paid For Your Sin???
That Which Is Hidden And Untold
Allow HIM To Unfold
HIS TRUTH For Your Situation.
That HE Might Perfect
HIS NEW CREATION!!!

HESED
John 4:1-26 & 2 Corinthians 5:17

REVERSAL OF PRIORITIES

Trying To Make Ends Meet?
When HE Said To Sit At HIS FEET!
Sit At HIS FEET And WAIT.
HE Is Never Late.
For That Which
HE Wants Us To Know~
HE Is Well Able To Bestow~
Knowledge~ Wealth And Health Too
Mercies All From
YESHUA ~ JESUS THE JEW.

HESED
Isaiah 40:31

SQUARE ONE

As Long As You Focus
On Square One Of
"The Problem."
You Leave Out The ONE
Who Can Do The "Solvin'!!"
GIVE HIM PRAISE
You Then HE Will Raise
Right To A Higher Height
Above Square One
This Is GOD'S Way Through
JESUS HIS SON.
HE Gives You Light
Even Delight In The Midst
Of "It" All~ It Is Just That On
JESUS You Must Needs Call.

HESED

TO LEARN HIS WAYS

A Time of SEPARATION~
A Time of PRAISE~
A Time of PREPARATION~
A Time of REPARATION~
A Time To BE with HIM~
Who is Without Sin
To LEARN HIS WAYS
For These LAST DAYS!!

HESED
2 Timothy 3:1

HE HAS ALL POWER!!

A Man's Foes
May Be Those Of
His Own "Household.".
GOD Knows The "Throes"
You May Be Going Through
Look To HIM
In The NAME Of
JESUS THE JEW.
HE Has ALL Power
To Change ~ Re-Arrange~
Think It Not Strange
Concerning the Fiery Trial!!
Within of THIS ~ There Is
No Denial ~ That
HE Is Training You For
A Greater Knowledge
Of HIMSELF~
That You Might Be Rich
In HIS WEALTH..

HESED~(Heb. GOD'S GRACE And MERCY)
Matthew 10:36 - 1 Peter 4:12-14

TO "GIVE UP" TO "GET"

You've Got To Give Up
What You've "Got"
To "Get" What HE'S Got.
Every Time You Sit Down
Lie Down ~ "Give Up!!"
You Give The "Enemy"
An Invitation To
Come In With His "Package"
Of Pain And Defeat;
When You Could Be
On Your Knees In Prayer.
JESUS IS THERE!
KING Of The Universe
Is HE. HE Came To Set
The Captive FREE!

HESED
Isaiah 61:1

A WATERED SEED

What They Need Is
That HOLY GHOST "HUG."
LOVE That Will Dissolve
The Heart Of A "Thug"
JESUS~ HE KNOWS
Just What They Need
In Their Heart
There Is A SEED
That Was Planted By
One Of The SAINTS Of GOD.
Now To Be WATERED
Without Restraint
By You ~ One Of HIS SAINTS.

HESED

WILHEMINA

Wilhemina~ She Said
She Was Mean
Until ~ JESUS She Had Seen.
HE Changed Her Life
Brought It Together.
She Now Stands In HIM
Through Any Weather!
Whether The Storm Is On
The Inside Or On The Outside
JESUS Gives HIS PEACE
HE Says, "Be Still."
As You Are
You Will KNOW HIS WILL!!!

HESED
Psalm 46:10 & Mark 4:39
Luke 10:38-42

WAYS MADE AVAILABLE

Look At Those Cattle
On A Thousand Hills
Don't You Think
HE Can Pay Those Bills?
HE Has Ways
We Know Not Of.
Ways Made Available
To HIS Beloved.
Call On HIM.
Do Not Wait!
HE Is Never Late.
JESUS THE CHRIST
Who Paid
The Greatest Price
For Our Salvation.
HIS BLOOD Was Shed For
Those From Every Nation.
To Clear The Sin Debt ~
The Biggest Debt Of All ~
For Us All.

HESED
Leviticus 17:11 & Psalm 50:10
Hebrews 9:11-14 & 22

HIS TOKEN

You Must Go On
What You Know
HE Has Spoken.
It Is HIS TOKEN
For "Success."
GOD'S BEST!!!
Not On What
You Think!
Then The Enemy
Will "Wink" At Any
Declension~
That Time You Did Not
Pay Attention To HIM~
JESUS And HIS "DIRECTIVES"
HIS HOLY GHOST
"CORRECTIVES."

HESED

PERSEVERENCE

Stick To GOD'S COURSE ~
No Remorse Then.
Hezekiah Did When~
His Death Sentence Was Given~
GOD'S MOTIVATION For Him
To Get Rid Of That Leaven.
Elijah Prayed~
Had To Check Seven Times
Before He Saw That Rain.
Daniel Too Had To Pray ~
Three Times A Day
Despite The King's Edict Not To.
Then GOD Could Act For Him Too.
Also That Answer For Him Was Delayed
Twenty One Days~
But GOD Came Through.
Perseverence Is Required HIS WORKS To Do.
Not To Forget GOD'S APPOINTED TIME~
Tho' It Tarry~
Wait For The Vision To Come.
The One Hundred And Twenty Had To

To Be Empowered For GOD'S WORK To Do.
Check Habakkuk Chapter Two.
Vision Directed~ You Avoid The Strain.
With The Vision HE Gives To You~
HE Will Accompany It With HIS POWER To Do.
With This Vision~ You Will Not Perish.
Stay With It!! If HIS PEOPLE You Would Nourish.
Remember Tho'~ Though It Tarry Wait!!
YESHUA~ JESUS ~HE Is Never Late!

HESED
1 Kings 18:41-44 ~Proverbs 29:18~ Isaiah 38:1~
Habakkuk 2:3 & Daniel 6:10 & 10:11-14

NOW

NOW Is The Time
When I Will Pour.
NOW Is The Time
To Look For MORE!!
NOW Is The Time When
 I Will Settle That "Score."
That Which Has Nettled
 from "Yore."
NOW Is The Time
For You To Look Unto ME.
NOW Is The Time
 I Will Hear Your Plea~
I AM JESUS THE CHRIST
YESHUA HA YEHUDI.
NOW Is The Time
For Your Kin To Come "In."
Have I Not Died For Their Sin??
NOW Is The Time
To BOW Before Destruction~
Even Those Under "Construction!!"
I Will Elevate You~
Look Unto ME~
This WORK To Do
NOW Is The Time ~

Psalm One Hundred And Two
A SET TIME To Favor Zion ~
The LAND Of The Jew~
This Time Has Been Set
By The MASTER~ "Time Keeper"
HE Would Have You Go
Deeper ~In Outreach
Deeper In HIM
Lengthen Those Cords Of Your Tent~
And HE Will Strengthen ~
As You Bring Them In.
You Have To Go Through Something
To Get to "NOW."
"NOW" Implies A Time Of Favor
GOD~ HE Has Seen Your Behaviour.
HE Notes A Savor In You
Your SAVIOUR~ JESUS THE CHRIST
YESHUA THE JEW~ A Reflection Of
HIS PERFECTION.
You Have Gone Through
That Trial Of
HOLY GHOST "Detection."
NOW Out Of Dejection~
HE Has Heard Your CRY!!!
HE Will Supply For Your Need.

Check Philippians 4:19.
Only To Pray~ GOD~
Will YOU "Speed??
HIS WORK Must Get DONE!!
THE HARVEST IS READY.
The Bales In The Fields
Have Been Rolled
How Many Have you Told ??
Lead To That ROLE??
That Which Is Being Written~
THE LAMB'S BOOK OF LIFE.
HOLY GHOST~ JESUS~ GOD
NEW LIFE!!!!!!!

HESED
Psalm 102:13-16 & Isaiah 54:2 & Matthew 9:37-38
Mark 4:29 & Luke 10:2 & John 4:35
Revelation 20:12-15 & 21:27

HIS SPECIAL SHEEP

As You Are Obedient
HE Will Keep
Even When The Way
Is Steep.
Has HE Not Said
HE Neither Slumbers
Nor Sleeps ~
Over ISRAEL
HIS Special Sheep~
Or You Out There
Who Have Been
Grafted In ~ Forgiven
Into The Commonwealth
Of HIM JESUS THE CHRIST
YESHUA THE JEW.
Over You ~ HIS CHOSEN
HE Will Watch Too.

HESED
Psalm 121:4 & Matthew 15:24
Ephesians 2:12-22 & Romans 11:15-36
Hebrews 13:5

SHORTS

LIFE'S LESSONS

This Is A Repeat
To Help You Get
On Your Feet.

HESED

CONFIDENCE

Confidence
Cast It Not Away.
For It Will Have
Great RECOMPENSE
Of Reward.
Look Not
At That Which Is
Untoward.
CONFIDENCE!
JESUS ~YESHUA
HE IS LORD.

HESED
Hebrews 10:35

CORRECTION

Will You Receive
CORRECTION??
Or Will You Call It
REJECTION??!!

HESED

RESTITUTION

As GOD Enabled
Restitution Between
Your Father And Brother
It Is Not Too Late~
To Beseech HIM
To Cause A
RESTITUTION
With Your Mother..

HESED
Acts 16:31
Household Salvation

WHATEVER

Whatever The Cause
Of Your Distress
Come To JESUS
You Will Be Blessed.
HESED

PREACHING

To Hear About
What Will Be.
And to Get Ready
For Eternity.
HESED

DEBIT

Not For Anyone
To Get The Credit.
It Is To JESUS
We Owe Our Debit!!
HESED

THIS IS THAT

This Is That Which
HE Hath Said.
It Is By HIS SPIRIT
We Must Be Lead.

HESED
Romans 8:14

FINAL DESTINATION

Remember
Your Final
DESTINATION.
It Is More Important
Your Present
"Inclination!"

HESED

WHEN

When You Diverge
From The LORD
HIS WILL And HIS WAY.
You Give The Enemy
An Open Invitation
To Come In And "Play!"

HESED

GOD

There Is No Other Way
For Me To Stand
Before YOU~
But By The Sacrifice Of
JESUS THE JEW.

HESED

COME APART

"Come Apart"
Words Of JESUS –
Given To Me.
"Come Apart"
That You May See.
"Come Apart" Before
You Come Apart!
This Word May Come
As A "Dart" To You~
But It Came From
The Heart Of
JESUS THE JEW.

YOUR TETHER

In Any Weather~
Look To JESUS
HE IS Your
 "Tether."
HE Will Keep You
Together!!

HESED
Isaiah 26:3

FORSAKING ALL

Forsaking All Is
What HE Said
That You Might
Not Be Mislead.

WHEREWITHAL
With GOD'S CALL
You Have HIS
WHEREWITHAL.

HESED
Philippians 4:19

GOD SPEED
Clarify The "Need."
Then It Will Be
GOD Who Will Give
You HIS "SPEED!!"

HESED
Philippians 4:6

FEAR NOT

Fear Not!!
Be Strong!!
With JESUS
You Cannot
Go "Wrong."

HESED
Deuteronomy 31:6
Joshua 1:9

NEVER LATE

Much For You To Assimilate
As On HIM You Wait!!
HE Is NEVER LATE!!!!

HESED
Isaiah 40:31

BALLADS

RE. THOMAS

Thomas Was A Jew
And Filled With Unbelief.
"Except I Shall See!!!"
John 20:25~
The Compassion, The REALITY
From GOD'S ONLY SON!!!
GOD'S KORBAN~SACRIFICE
For All Men~ To Know HIM
How Much Will You Spend??
For That Pearl Of Great Price~
JESUS THE CHRIST~
YESHUA THE JEW
This Is A Question HE Could
Ask Of You ~And HE Too
Would Reply ~ As HE Did "Then"
Only Believe!! I AM THE ONE
Who Came For The SALVATION
Of ALL MEN!!!!!!!!!!!!!!!!!!

HESED
Matthew 13:45-46

Note~ HIS LIFE Was Freely Given For
You Is It Not Time To Consider "This"
With Eternity In View??!!!!

GOD WANTS TO SHOW YOU SOMETHING

GOD Wants To Show
You Something
It Is At Your Door
HE'S Been "Thumping."
"Thumping" For You
To Let HIM Come IN.
JESUS CHRIST Said:
"Ye Must Be BORN AGAIN."
"Then I Will Come And
Sup With You~
Give You A Life Like
You Never Knew.
You Will Never Hunger.
You Will Never Thirst~
As Long As You Put
ME First."

HESED
Matthew 6:31-34
John 3:3 & 5 & 7 & 16 & 6:35

NEHEMIAH

Nehemiah He Was
Higher Up Than Most.
He Was Lead by
The HOLY GHOST.
To Rebuild He Was
Determined.
Even Though The Enemy
Poured Out His Vermin.
In One Way Or Another~
But Nehemiah Undeterred
Continued~ Even As
The Devil Stirred.
The Wall He Built
And So Today~
This Is What
GOD Would Say:
Am I Not The Same
As I Was Then?
I Sent JESUS That
You Might Be
"BORN AGAIN."

Walls Rebuilt
That Have Been Broken Down
That In That Last Day~
You Might Have A Crown!

HESED
Nehemiah 4~Hebrews 13:8 & John 3:7

GOD'S THRUST

GOD Provided A Ram
For Abraham.
HE Provided HIS SON For Us.
THIS Was GOD'S THRUST.

That We Might Be
REDEEMED.
In That Last Day
With HIM Seen..

Abraham's Son Spared
And So Are We~
To Choose For Eternity
I.e. Where It Will be.

Choose You This Day
Whom You Will Serve.
Abraham Heard
GOD'S Voice And Obeyed.

Let It Not Be Said Of You
That You Delayed!!
JESUS THE CHRIST ~
YESHUA THE JEW

HE Has Loved All Mankind
Including You~That
You Might Not Be Blind ~
To THIS TRUTH.

HE Was "The WAY"
Is Now And Will Be.
The WORD Made Flesh For
All To See.

HESED
Genesis 22~Joshua 24:15
John 1:14 & John 14:6

AT THAT WORD!!!

GOD Has HIS "Goad"
Behind You.
Whatever HE Says
You Must Needs "DO!!."
At That WORD ~
Water Was Turned Into Wine.
At THAT WORD
Rain Fell On Carmel.
Tho' Seven Times
Elijah Looked And Hoped
He Later Received Of
GOD'S SCOPE
That Which HE Said
HE Would Do~ Patience ~
HE HAD NOT LIED
Patience Was Needed
For GOD'S WILL
To Be Satisfied..

HESED
Numbers 23:19 ~1 Kings 18:17-46
Habakkuk 2:3 ~ John 2:1-11
Acts 5:39 & 9:5

GOD'S RESCUE

Moses Was Taken From The Water.
Pharaoh's Wife Did Not Falter~
Did Not Hesitate To
Remove Him There-from
And So It Is With
GOD'S ONLY SON ~Whom
HE Has Sent.
For Man's SALVATION
GOD Was Bent.
Joseph Was Rescued From
The Pit And Prison.
JESUS From Death Has Risen.
GOD'S Victory In These Situations
That Man Might Become HIS
NEW CREATION.

HESED
2 Corinthians 5:17

GIDEON AND ABRAHAM

Gideon- He Heard GOD'S VOICE
And Accepted "The Commission."
After He Put Out A Fleece Or Two.
GOD HIMSELF Then Charged His "Ignition"
But Gideon Had To Downsize His Group
Three Hundred Became
The Size Of His Troop.....
With "Those" GOD Was Responsible For
"The Outcome".........The Battle Was Won.
Abraham Was Given A Choice Of The Land
That Was To Be Occupied..
His Brother Lot Was In The Plan-
He Chose Sodom- The "Bottom"
As It Turned Out To Be. There Were
Not Even Ten Righteous In That City.
Sodomy Was Rampant. It Did Abound.
From There Lot Was Warned To Flee.
He Obeyed And Did Not See
What Happened To His Wife Who Did
Look Back.... MOST IMPORTANT
Then As Now Not To Look Back Or
Ask GOD How?? HE Is Omniscient

And Looks For Our Trust... Then We
Are Ready For "HIS THRUST.."

HESED
Genesis 13:8-13 & 19:15-29
Judges 6:39-40 & Chapter 7

BUT MICAH
FOR MICAH

Micah Was Born In Israel
I Am Told
BUT Micah
HE Became Enamored For
America's Gold!!!
Job After Job He Tried
But Micah
He Was Not Satisfied
To Return To THE LAND
Was Not On His Agenda~
He Had Another~ You See.
But Then One Day
Came A Knock At His Door
What About ME???

If You Want "More??"
"Well I Have A House
And A Wife And A Car!!"
"BUT" ~ HE Says~
"What I Have Relates
To You
Right Where You Are.
COME UNTO ME~
With All Of Those
Intentions~
Even Those Not Mentioned
And I Will Give You
A New "Dimension!!"
JESUS THE CHRIST
YESHUA THE JEW
From The Beginning
I Have Known About You.
You See Psalm 139
For A Verity~
With A Love I Have Seen
And Love You Still~
I Am Even Ready To Pay
Your "Bills!!"
COME UNTO ME.
Your Cup I Will Fill."

HESED
Deuteronomy 20:1-8
Psalm 23:5 ~Matthew 11:28
Luke 14:16-19

Revelation 3:20

A Name-Change Was Involved
That The Question Of Anonymity
Might Be Resolved.

DALET AND DELET

Dalet Is Number Four
In The Hebrew Alphabet
Through The Delet~ The Door
Your Needs Will Be Met!!
YESHUA Is Your Door For
Eternal Life~ HE Is THE ONE
Who Can Rid You Of Strife.
YESHUA~ The Fourth Man
In That Fiery Furnace~
Way Back When Daniel Was
In That Lion's Den.
Now YESHUA
Will Come Back Soon~

The Lion From The Tribe Of Judah.
In Isaiah He Wrote Of HIM
That HE Came To Set The
Captive Free~ See Isaiah 61
Before In Isaiah 53~ HE Was
Already Wounded For Our
Transgressions~ So Many
Lessons To Learn~ Most
Important Not To Spurn
HIS LOVE For You
JESUS THE CHRIST
YESHUA THE JEW.

HESED- Heb. GOD'S GRACE & MERCY
Isaiah 53:5~Isaiah 61:1
Daniel Chapter 3
John 10:9 ~Revelation 5:5
Dalet~ Heb. Number Four
Delet~ Heb. Door

P.S. Isaiah Said HE Would Be
Born Of A Virgin Chapter Seven
Verse Fourteen~ And In Chapter
Nine Verse Six~ HE IS
THE PRINCE OF PEACE
With The Government On HIS
SHOULDERS~ So Many Boulders

We Need To Allow HIM To Move
For Us~ That In HIM We May
Come To Truly TRUST!!!!!!!!

MERCIES WITH YESHUA

Mordecai And Joseph~
Both were Put Aside
That GOD'S PLAN
Might Be Satisfied.
In Due Time
GOD Came Through.
HE Caused Men To
Remember The JEW.
The Jew Who Was
Forgotten In Prison.
The Jew Who
Wouldn't Bow Down.
For This Reason
His Name (Mordecai)
Was Written Down;
Because He Had Done
Something "Good" Before.
For This GOD Opened

The Door.
GOD Gave Him Favor
With The King.
Thereafter He Could Sing!
Esther Was Queen And
His Position Was Elevated
No Question ~It Was Not
Debated.
GOD Came Through!!
As HE Has in The Past
HE Will Again Too.
GOD Careth For The Jew.
HIS Eyes Are Not Shut.
For ISRAEL~
HE Does Not Slumber.
Mercies With YESHUA
They Are Without Number!!!

HESED
Genesis 41: 38-43
Esther 10:2-3
Psalm 121:4 & Hebrews 13:8

AS THE ISRAELITES

As The Israelites
Looked To The Serpent
And Were Healed.
GOD In This Day Has
Those Who Are
HOLY GHOST SEALED!!
Sealed With THE PROMISE
Looking Unto HIM~
BORN AGAIN~ Healed Too
Ready For The Coming Of
JESUS THE JEW.
And For "More"
Whatever "The Score"
HE Is Their DOOR.
Again For Healing Too~
Repealing The Works
The Serpent Would Try To Do.
The Serpent Evil~ The Devil
Incarnate BUT
With JESUS We Have
A "Helmet"~
HIS SALVATION~

Available To Those From
Every Nation~
For Each One Who Will
B E C O M E
That New Creation Through
GOD'S ONLY SON~
JESUS THE CHRIST
YESHUA THE JEW.

HESED
Numbers 21:5-9 & Acts 28:3-6 ~
Ephesians 1:11-14 & 6:17
John 3:3 & 16 & John 10:9
2 Corinthians 5:17

ABRAHAM BUT!!!!!

Abraham- Was Willing
To Sacrifice His Son~
But GOD Had Another ONE.
For This Reason Then~
HE Sent The Ram~
A Foreshadowing
Of HIS ETERNAL PLAN.
The LAMB Slain Before
The Foundation Of The World.

Without The Shedding Of Blood
There Is No Remission For
Sin~ Leviticus Said It (Ch. 17)
The Blood Of Bulls & Goats
Did Not Atone~
For That Reason God Sent
HIS OWN~ A Living Sacrifice Ie
To Identify With Humanity
In Its Fallen State Yet
To Mediate- "Kaparati"
A Covering Has Been Provided For
YESHUA~ HE IS THE DOOR.

HESED
Genesis 22:13 & Revelation 13:8
Behold The LAMB OF GOD That
Taketh Away The Sin Of The World...John 1:29
For All Have Sinned...Romans 3:23

Kaparati~Heb. My Covering

HIS PLANS

David Asked Of
THE LORD ~ A Sign
When His Very Life
Was At Stake...
MOSES Said I Will Not
Go~ Unless YOU
Go Before Me~
Gideon Needed Assurance Too
He Set Out A Fleece
And Then He Knew.
The Dew ie. Watered
The Fleece~ Then
The Ground Around
And Then He Knew GOD Would
Deliver Israel Into His
Hands~
GOD'S PROVISION~
HIMSELF SUFFICIENT
For HIS PLANS!!

HESED
Exodus 3:11-15 ~Judges 6:36-40
1 Samuel 20:11-42

FULL LIFE

Faster Than A Computer ~
Faster Than Your Brain ~
All JESUS Asks Of You Is
That You Ask
HIM To Reign ~
Reign In Your Life
Then You Will See
What It Is A FULL LIFE
Can Be!

HESED

ISRAEL GOD'S PLAN

Behold HE That Keepeth Israel
Shall Neither Slumber Nor Sleep.
Psalm 121:4

The LORD Shall Yet Comfort Zion
And Shall Yet Choose Jerusalem.
Zechariah 1:17

No Place On Earth Has A Specific
Promise For Its Well-Being ie.
From GOD Who Is All-Seeing!!

E X C E P T ~ I S R A E L!!   HESED

PSALM 102:16

When The LORD Shall Build Up Zion, HE Shall Appear In HIS GLORY.

ZECHARIAH 2:8

…He That Touches You Touches The Apple Of GOD'S EYE.

ZECHARIAH 12:9

And It Shall Come To Pass In That Day, That I Will Seek To Destroy All Nations That Come Against Jerusalem.

PSALM 132:13

For The Lord Hath Chosen Zion; HE Hath Desired It For His Habitation.

NOTE!!

America!! Israel!!~Hear!! GOD'S WORD To You
The "Piece" Process Will Not Work~ For It Is
HIS PLAN You Shirk~ HE Gave The Land To The
Jew~ Not For You To Divide As Something "New!!!"

HESED

GOD HAS A PLAN!!

Re. The Peace Process~
GOD Has The Plan ~
Another One
It All Has To Do With
GOD'S Only SON~ ie.
THE PRINCE OF PEACE
HE'S Called~
No Wonder
The "Process" Has
Stalled!!!!
GOD'S PLAN
For THE LAND
HE Gave It To The Jew.
Read GOD'S WORD
 If This Does Not
Make "Sense" To You.
Then You Will See
GOD'S View.
Without HIS "INFUSION"
You Bring A Contusion
To THE LAND And
To Your Own Soul.
With HIM~ HIS PEACE
Will Make Whole.

Whole In The Soul
WHOLE For THE LAND
Before GOD On This
I Will STAND~
Check Isaiah 53 And 9:6
For Peace GOD'S "FIX!!"

HESED

PIECE ~ PEACE!!!

WHAT IS PEACE WITH "THEM??"
The Palestinian!!

With Civil War (*Eminent*) *Within??!!*
Peace! Peace And "Then
Sudden Destruction!!"
This Piece~ Peace Process
Is A High Price To Pay For
THE LAND ~ Under CONSTRUCTION
With MESSIAH On The Way
Is It Not Time To Get Ready
HIS WAY???
Check In THE BOOK Again
Re. HIS PLAN For THE LAND.
HE Is Not Willing That Any Should
Perish ~ Nor For A Give-Up Of

THE LAND HE Would Have
You CHERISH!!!

HESED
Psalm 69:35 ~ Psalm 102:16
Psalm 147:12-14
John 3:16 ~ 1 Thessalonians 5:3

THE ISSUE OF BLOOD

Israel Is Like The Woman
With The Issue Of Blood.
Her Issue Continued For
Twelve Years~ Then.
Now~ Israel Like The Woman
Has A Problem~ Hers With Men.
Pleasing Them~ The World ie.
At The Expense Of Her Very
Existence~ For Which She
Could No Longer Pay!! You See~
You See!!! May GOD Yet Have
Mercy That Israel Might Realize
That Man's Plan Without HIS
Is A Pack Of Lies!!!!
JESUS~ YESHUA Shed

HIS BLOOD For The "Whole Deal"
That Unto HIM The World
Might Come And Be Healed ie.
To JESUS THE CHRIST
YESHUA HA YEHUDI.

HESED
Matthew 9:20~ Mark 5:25-34
Luke 8:43-48

ZION!! FOR WHAT??

Zion For What Are You Cryin'??
The LORD Has Not Forsaken You !!
You Are Graven On The Palms Of
H I S   H A N D S!!
Tho' To You ~ This May Be
A New View~
It Comes From The Heart Of
JESUS~ YESHUA The Jew.
You Must Needs Look In THE BOOK
For HIS PLANS For You~
Then GOD HIMSELF

Will Manifest To You VIA
That Which Is TRUE!!

HESED
Isaiah 49:13-16 & John 14:6 & 20:25

THAT GREEN SPRIG!!

See That Green Sprig?? That One Blade!!!
Coming Up Out Of The Ground??
Through This GOD Says HE Is Still Around!!
Wonders!! GOD Has Chosen That
Which Is Foolish To Confound The Wise~
JESUS Only Can Open Man's Eyes!

HESED
1 Corinthians 1:25

*I Saw This "Blade" Coming Up Out Of The Most
Parched~ Sun-Dried Ground In November @ The
New Settlement Of Modiin In ISRAEL*

THAT YOUR PEOPLE

GOD – Even This Night
We Are Calling To YOU.
That The Plight Of
Our People May Be
Brought To View,
That The Plan Of
The Enemy Might
Be Put To Flight
That Your PEOPLE
Might Not Be
Forever "Up-Tight."

HESED

*Scuds- Explosive Devices- ie
Vices Of The Enemy!!!! ISRAEL*

HOLY HUDSPA!!

HOLY HUDSPA Is What You've Got
GOD HIMSELF Has Seen Your Lot~
HE Is Pleased For All Of HIS On Their Knees.
Difficulties In THE LAND
GOD'S SPAN For HIS PLAN~
HOLY HUDSPA Is Needed To Not Accede
To The Lies And Torment Of The Enemy~
With HOLY HUDSPA For YESHUA/JESUS
Therein Is The VICTORY!!!~ NITZAHONE!!!
HA DAM SHEL YESHUA Does Atone!!
As In Reverence And With
HOLY SUPPLICATION
You Come Unto HIM~ JESUS THE CHRIST
YESHUA THE JEW~ Great Works Attested To!!

HESED
See- Zechariah 2:8~ John 14:12

HUDSPA~ Heb. Boldness~ ("Nerve"~ Courage)
HA DAM SHEL YESHUA ~ Heb. THE BLOOD Of JESUS
Nitzahone~ Heb. Victory!!

LOOK YOU ARABS AND YOU JEWS

Look You Arabs And You Jews
You Can Get Together
That's The Good News!!
There's Only One Mediator
Between GOD And Man.
To Bring Redemption
That's GOD'S PLAN.
JESUS CHRIST~ GOD'S SON
Shed HIS BLOOD That You Might Not.
HIS BLOOD Can Cleanse Each Spot.
A Spot Of Sin~ A Spot Of Hate~
It Is To HIM~ You Need Relate.
COME TO JESUS Before HIM BOW.
HE LOVES YOU BOTH.
Do IT Right Now!!

HESED

HUMANLY SPEAKING

Humanly Speaking Neither "One Side"
Is "Better" Than The Other~
For All Have Sinned And Come Short Of The
Glory Of GOD~ Romans 3:23
The Palestinians Want You To Be Sorry
For Their Plight~ Those Who Are Not To
The Far Right~ *Hamas~ Hezbullah Etc.*
The Israelis Want You To Know All
The Good They Do~ True!!
BUT!!! Without JESUS~YESHUA
In Their Hearts~ What Can Either
Side Do???????????
Humanity Is In A Fallen State.
Even At Its Moral Best!!
Only With JESUS~ YESHUA
Can Anyone Pass "The Test!!"
GOD HAS A PLAN~ ONLY "THAT"
Will Stand.
GOD HIMSELF Is Going To Turn
HIS LIGHT TO ISRAEL~ TO THE JEW
And In Their Favor.
From That Nation HE Sent THE SAVIOUR.
Coming Back Soon!!
The Gentiles Need To Get "In Tune!!!!"

While They Have A Chance
Lest Before Al-Quaida~ Or
The Anti Christ They Will Be Called To Dance.
Only JESUS~ YESHUA Is Sufficient For Either "Side"
Without HIM There Is No Place To Hide!!
So Come To HIM Now !!
No More "Cow-Towing!!!"
It Is Before HIM We ALL Will Be Bowing.

HESED
Philippians 2:10 & Revelation 6:12-17

To YOUR WILL Now "Mine!!" Lest At The Last Day
It Will Be Said By THE SAVIOUR "To ME You Did Not Incline!!"
With A Prayer You Can Get Ready~ GOD HIMSELF
Will Hold You Steady~ If This Is Your True Inclination.
HE HIMSELF IS THE AUTHOR OF SALVATION
To Each Nation~ The Jew Included~ Lest Anyone Be
Deluded!

HESED

BEHOLD THE LAMB OF GOD WHICH TAKETH AWAY
THE SIN OF THE WORLD~ *John 1:29*

RE. THE ARAB & THE JEW

They Were Together "Then."
Genesis 25:9 ~ Genesis 35:29

They Came From The Same
Father...

In YESHUA They Will Go
Back To The Same Father..

HE Made "THIS" Possible ie.
JESUS THE CHRIST
YESHUA HA YEHUDI...

P.S. There "Can" Be Peace
Even In The "Middle-East"
Isaiah 9:6
The PRINCE OF PEACE
HE Is Called..
Not Much Time ~On This "Point"
To Stall~ HE Is Coming Soon.
Time For Us All To Get
Stay~Be ~ "In-Tune."

HESED
Genesis 35:29 ~ Isaiah 53
Psalm 107:13 & 15-31

GOD ~WILL NOT FORSAKE ISRAEL!!!!

ISAIAH 43:21-22

This People Have I Formed For MYSELF They
Shall Show Forth MY PRAISE. But Thou Hast Not
Called Upon ME, O Jacob; Thou Hast Been Weary
Of ME O ISRAEL.

ISAIAH 49:14-15

But Zion said The LORD Hath Forsaken Me,
And My LORD Hath Forgotten Me.
Can A Woman Forget Her Sucking Child,
That She Should Not Have Compassion
On The Son Of Her Womb? Yea They
May Forget, Yet Will I Not Forget Thee.

PSALM 130:7-8

Let ISRAEL Hope In The LORD: For With
The LORD There Is Mercy, And With HIM
Is Plenteous Redemption. And HE Shall
Redeem ISRAEL From All His Iniquities.

PRAYER

THE AHMADINEJAD CRISIS
THE U.S. ~ ISRAEL IN CRISIS

GOD YOU Are Swifter
Than A Plane.
Swifter Than A Fax.
When The Enemy
Comes In Like A Flood~
YOU Are There With
YOUR Ax. The Ax Of
The HOLY SPIRIT
On Location~ Near It~
That Situation~About To Explode!!
GOD YOU Have
YOUR Load Of Weapons~
YOUR Arsenal~YOUR Servants
In Prayer.
For "That" Situation~
YOU Care!! YOU Spare~
For That Taken In Issue~
Taken To YOU IN PRAYER.

HESED
Isaiah 59:19

I LOOKED FOR

I Looked For An
Intercessor
One To Stand In
The Gap.
Too Many Were
Taking A Nap.
Too Many Were
Away From "The Map"
The "Map" Of
GOD'S WORD.
They Were Deterred.
BUT ~ Then By
The WORD
They Were Recalled
Brought Back
From Where
They Had Stalled.
To Where GOD'S WORD
Would "Stir" In Them.
That They Might
Recommence To Become
Fishers Of Men.

HESED
Ezekiel 22:30- 1 Thessalonians 5:17

IN PRAYER

It Is In Prayer
That I Must Be.
Then I Can See
What HE Does
Require Of Me.
Trying To Fulfill
In Your Own Way?
What Only GOD
Can Fulfill
As You Pray.

THIS IS WHERE

This Is Where
The Gospel Is Preached.
This Is Where
Souls Are Reached.
In The Sanctuary
On The Street ~
First We Must
Spend Time At
JESUS' FEET.

HESED

"PRESS!!!"

Take His Promise!!
Press And Prevail!!
Or Sit Back ~ Do Nothing
Let The Enemy Avail ?!!!
Your Choice.
Listen To His Voice.
With Him ~ You Win!
JESUS CHRIST~GOD'S SON.
His Work Is Done!!
Now For You To
Follow Through.
Press And ~
You Will Be Blessed.

HESED
Philippians 3:14

THOU ONLY.....

"WARFARE"~ IT'S PRAYER!!
HOLY GHOST~ Infiltrate!!
Propitiate~ Mitigate!
Alleviate~ ABBREVIATE
The Plan Of The Enemy..
That Which Is Not Of "THEE."
THOU ONLY KNOWEST
What In That "Plan" Is True..
THOU ONLY Can Expose
That Which Is Hidden
And Bring It To View..
As Before YOU We Bow
To Punctuate In The "Now"
HOLY GHOST~ "KNOW HOW."
Ie. How To Pray In Sincerity
Against This Plot Of The Enemy
In The NAME Of
JESUS THE CHRIST
YESHUA HA YEHUDI.......

HESED

*I Will Worship Toward Thy Holy Temple, And Praise THY
NAME For Thy Loving-Kindness And For Thy Truth: For Thou
Hast Magnified Thy Word Above All Thy Name. Psalm 138:2*

*GOD Gave Solomon Wisdom- We Need It Too...Note The
Discernment Given "Then" In THE LAND Of The Jew*

PURIM

Purim~ GOD KNOWS
What HE Is "Doin.' "
Way Back "Then."
Esther Fasted~ The
Plan Of The Enemy
Was "Blasted."
And So Today
Ought We Not To Fast And
Pray~ GOD Is Able To
Deliver Again.
When The Enemy Comes
In Like A Flood~
THE BLOOD ~As At
Passover Is HIS SIGN
HE Is There To Atone
HE Is LORD Of Lords
To HIS OWN.
Purim ~ The Passover
Of HIM We Sing
JESUS THE CHRIST
YESHUA THE JEW
GOD'S DELIVERER
SAVIOUR For Me And You.

HESED

Exodus 12:13 ~Esther 4:16 ~ Isaiah 59:15
John 1:29~ 1 Corinthians 5:7~Revelation 19:16

PURIM~ JEWISH HOLIDAY~ Early Spring

RE. RAIN

Repentance Is Needed~Prior
For Any Prayer To "Go Through."
This Is GOD'S PRESCRIPTION
Through JESUS THE JEW~
Corporate Agreement Thereunto
According To THE WORD.
GOD'S ATTENTION Is Stirred.
Rain Is One Of HIS Concerns Too.
Though Perseverence May Be Needed
For Your Prayer To Go Through.
Elijah Prayed Seven Times Before
He Saw That Rain… GOD Who Is
The Same Today As HE Was Yesterday
Can Send It (Rain) Again…
This Time Now~Pray In
JESUS'~YESHUA'S NAME.

HESED
1 Kings 8:33-36 & 18:41-44
2 Chronicles 6:26-27 & 7:13-14
Jeremiah 5:22-25 & Amos 4:7-8
Hebrews 13:8 & Matthew 18:20

INTERCESSION

The GOD OF ISRAEL
Will Hear Your Cry.
As You DEFY
The Enemies Of
THE LIVING GOD~
And Their Plan
Against THE SON OF MAN.
CRY OUT FOR THE LOST!
CRY OUT FOR THE LAND!
It Must Come Back
To HIS PEOPLE
Who Stand In Lack~
Lack Of Knowledge
Without HIM
Still In Sin.
STAND ON THE WALLS~
HIS PLACE Of Redoubt.
The WALLS OF INTERCESSION~
That Is For The Few
Who Make INTERCESSION
Through YESHUA ~
JESUS THE JEW.

HESED
Isaiah 59:16 & Ezekiel 33:7-16

BROTHERS

HE Was A Jew Then!
HE IS Now
In The Hearts Of Men.
HE Will Be
When HE Comes
Back Again!!
Men Who Can Believe
Will HIM RECEIVE.
They Will THEN
Not Grieve Themselves
Or Others.
With JESUS ~ YESHUA
In Their Hearts
They ARE BROTHERS!!

HESED
Mark 3:35
2 Corinthians 5:17

DANIEL'S PRAYER FOR JERUSALEM

DANIEL 9:18-19

O My GOD Incline Thine Ear, And Hear; Open Thine Eyes And Behold Our Desolations And The City Which Is Called By Thy Name For We Do Not Present Our Supplications Before Thee For Our Righteousnesses, But For THY Great Mercies.

O LORD, Hear; O LORD, Forgive; O LORD Hearken And Do: Defer Not, For Thine Own Sake, O My GOD: For THY City And THY People Are Called By THY NAME.

PSALM 122:6

6Pray For The Peace Of Jerusalem: They Shall Prosper That Love Thee.

In War Or Famine Let GOD Do The "Plannin.'"
HESED
Psalm 33:19

AMERICA ! ! !

AMERICA REPENT

The Black Man Has Been
Abused And Refused.
The White Man Has Rejected
The Good News!
The Jews Remain When
GOD Has Given Them A LAND
Where They Could Be
In GOD'S PLAN.
America ~ Wake Up!! Before
It's Too Late!!
Rome And Sodom
Had Their Fate!
There Is A SAVIOUR
GOD-GIVEN For ALL.
HIS NAME IS JESUS.
On HIM ~ You Need CALL!
Ninevah Was Smart.
It Took To Heart
GOD'S MESSAGE To Them
Through Jonah They Repented
America ~ You Can TOO!
REPENT~ RECEIVE SALVATION
Through JESUS THE JEW.

HESED
Genesis 19:20 & Amos 4:11 & Jonah 3:3-10

GLOBAL WARMING???!!!

"Global Warming??!!"
Is GOD'S Warning........
HE Can Turn It On
HE Can Turn It Off....
Lest You Scoff In Unbelief
What You Need Is Some
Good Grief~ ie Repentance
A Gift Which Can Be
Granted To You Through
JESUS THE CHRIST
YESHUA THE JEW.

HESED
Matthew 24:5-8 & Mark 13:5-8
& Luke 21:25-28

Earthquakes~ Volcanos Through Ice!
Mud Slides ~Tsunamis Etc..........

LOCKED?!

Locked
In The Land Of
Their Captivity
To The Dollar
And Their Stocks
GOD'S PEOPLE
Are Locked!
Locked From What
GOD Has For Them
They Need To Be
"BORN AGAIN"
Sins Forgiven ~
YOM KIPPUR
For Each One
YESHUA Is The
DOOR.

HESED
Micah 4:7
John 3:3 & 5 & 7 & 16
John 10:9~

American Jew Awake! There Is Going To Be A "SHAKE"
For GOD'S "TAKE"~ IMMIGRATE!~ HESED

LEST YOU FAINT!!

Lest You Faint
And Say:
"GOD "Ain't'" Around!!"
Check In HIS WORD
That The Plan Of
The Enemy To Your Soul
You Might Confound!!
By The Trust
You Place In HIS WORD~
The ONE WHO HAS
SAVED Your Soul!
JESUS THE CHRIST
YESHUA THE JEW.
HE Has Not
Forgotten You!!!

HESED
Psalm 124 & Isaiah 49:14-16

RE. WAR~
FOR HEADS OF STATE

If They Would Go To GOD
For HIS INSTRUCTIONS
There Would Be A Lot Less
Destruction!!!

HESED

PRAYER

In The "Middle"
Send Up "Tinder"
That None Can Hinder!
Even As Elijah Did
Against The Gods Of Baal
GOD YOU ONLY KNOW
How To "Curtail"
The Plan Of The Enemy.
ONLY YOU HAVE POWER
To Quell This "Insanity!!"
And Human Depravity
Of War~
GOD We Look To You
Whom We Adore

JESUS THE CHRIST
YESHUA THE JEW.
That Which Is "Slated"
To Happen~
To The Altar ~ Ourselves
We Are "Strappin."
For YOUR REVERSE
Of This "Curse."
When Man's Folly
Reaches Its Extremity
GOD With HIS POWER
Is In Close Proximity!!

HESED
1 Kings 18

When Man's Folly Reaches Its Extreme
GOD With HIS POWER Is SUPREME!!

HOLY DAYS ~ HOLIDAYS

PREFACE TO
THE PASSOVER COLLECTION

As GOD Allowed All Those Plagues In The Land Where HIS
PEOPLE Stayed So There Are Those Who May Have Strayed Or
Never Known HIM~
HE WHO Can Do It Again~ I.e. With Those Episodes You Are
Going Through~Illness~ Family Situations` HE Still Has POWER
To Deliver You!! JESUS THE CHRIST ~ YESHUA THE JEW.
In The Old Testament HE Said:"I Am The LORD That Healeth
Thee. "*Again There Is Nothing Too Difficult For HIM.
HE Gives The Power To Be BORN AGAIN! HE Who Calls You
To HIS "Marvelous Light!!" HE Who Is The "Light Of The
World" Though Satan's Darts At You May Be Hurled~
Again!! There Is Nothing Too Difficult For HE Who Died For
All Sin And Disease~ Read In The New Testament TOO So Many
Accounts Of Healing ~
Revealing So Much Of That Concealed. As HIS NAME Was Not
Before Revealed Ie. In The Old Testament YESHUA But NOW
HIS Anointed And Appointed:
THE CHRIST Isaiah 61 GOD'S ONLY SON.

HESED- Heb. GOD'S GRACE & MERCY
As Received by Barbara Knowles ©June 2004

Refs. *See Exodus 15:26 & Psalm 30:2~Jeremiah 32:17 & 27 ~ John 1:12 & John 3:7~ 1 Peter 2:9 ~John 8:12~ Ephesians 6:16~ John 3:16~ Isaiah 61:1-3~Luke 4:18

POEMS TO STUDY~ Check This Out!!! GOD Invariably Has And Knows Your Route See Psalm 139 & When You Do You Will See HE Is Alive Today TOO!!

A SIGN

The Passover And The Crucifixion
Have To Do With Blood.
The BLOOD Applied To The
Doorposts Of The Dwellings
Or The Tent Of Dwelling.
A Sign From GOD In Heaven
That That Which Has Been Covered
Was Protected ~ Was Forgiven.
Blood Over The Doorposts
On A Hyssop Stick Or
That Which Was Offered To
H I S   L I P S.
JESUS THE CHRIST
YESHUA THE JEW
Will You Allow HIM
GOD'S KORBAN~
PERFECT SACRIFICE
To Become IT For You??

HESED
Read Hebrews Chapter 9 & 10

Korban Heb. Sacrifice

NO MORE

No More Birds, Goats, Bullocks
Are Needed!!
Only The Prayer Of
THE ONE Who Has PLEADED
Will Be Answered. ~ Through HIM
HIM~ GOD'S PERFECT SACRIFICE
For All Sin.
No More Good Deeds To Atone
Only The SHED BLOOD Of THE ONE
Who Is Now Near THE THRONE
Of ELOHIM~ Seated THERE.
YESHUA~ JESUS Is THE ONE
Through WHOM GOD Will
Answer Your Prayer.
Call On HIM~ No More Dejection
Need You Tolerate As You Look
To HIM~ HE Will Operate~
Atone For Your Sin.
ENTER IN!!!!

HESED
Mark 16:19 ~ Ephesians 2:8-9
Hebrews 9:8-14~ Revelation 7:10

ELOHIM~Heb.~ GOD ~YESHUA~ JESUS

PASSOVER

Passover A Holy Celebration
Of A Divine Evacuation!!
A Holy Convocation
Much Deliberation To Recall
That In Future Years We
Might Not Stall In Apprehension
But Look To HIM Whose
Mercies We All Can Mention
JESUS THE CHRIST
YESHUA THE JEW.
GOD'S PASSOVER LAMB
For Each One Who Has Been
BORN AGAIN.

HESED
Note!! HE Wants To Manifest HIS SALVATION
For Every Situation!!

THE LAMB ~ GOD'S KORBAN

The I AM Sent THE LAMB.
The I AM Sent THE LAMB.
Hi! Ho! To YESHUA GO!!
YESHUA Was THE LAMB.
YESHUA Was GOD'S KORBAN.

GOD'S KORBAN Was Not The Ram
GOD'S KORBAN Was Not The Ram
Hi! Ho! To YESHUA GO!!
For Man~ GOD Sent THE LAMB.
YESHUA WAS HIS PLAN!!
YESHUA IS THE LAMB!!

HESED
Genesis 22:10-14 & John 1:29

Korban~ Heb.- Sacrifice & YESHUA~Heb~ JESUS
To The Tune Of "The Farmer In The Dell"

RIVEN

Riven ~ Forgiven
Riven~
HIS SIDE Was.
Forgiven~
My Sins Were Too
All Because Of~
JESUS THE JEW.
Without The
Shedding Of Blood
There Is No
Remission For Sin.
But HIS SIDE Was RIVEN.
That All Might Enter In.
RIVEN ~ FORGIVEN
Because Of HIM.

HESED
Leviticus 17:11 & Psalm 22:16
John 19:34-37 & Hebrews 9:22

TO "YANK"

Passover Time
Leg Bone Or The Shank
GOD Is Able To "Yank"..
That One Out Of The Fire.
For "This" HE Sent
T H E M E S S I A H.
Not A Bone Of HIS Was Broken
 GOD'S WORD
Was Not Either ~ Rather
It Was Fulfilled!!
JESUS HUNG ON THE CROSS
A Stigma For You??
SALVATION For Me!!
GOD'S ~ LAMB ~ KORBAN
Giving You Power To "Yank"
That One To See ~
There Has Been An Atonement
The BLOOD Has Been Shed
MESSIAH IS ALIVE~
HE Is Not Dead!!
Soon Coming Back~ No Need
To Live Your Life In Dread!!
"Fear Not" Said HE

Us To Free!!!!
JESUS THE CHRIST ~
YESHUA HA YEHUDI.

HESED
Psalm 34:20 ~ 1 Peter 4:12-14 ~Jude 23

Re. SIN: Sin Is Our Common Denominator
JESUS Is OUR MEDIATOR.
YESHUA ~ GEULA ~ JESUS ~ SALVATION
Who Frees From Sin That The Jew And The
Gentile Might Become Kin Ie.
BORN AGAIN. ~ John Chapter 3:3 & 5 & 7
GEULA ~ Heb ~Redemption ~ KORBAN ~ Sacrifice
YESHUA HA YEHUDI~ JESUS THE JEW

COME BACK!!!

"NOT MY WIILL BUT THINE BE DONE ~ Luke 22:42

Words From GOD'S ONLY SON.

MY GOD, My GOD, Why Hast THOU Forsaken ME? Mark 15:34

Words Spoken By HIM Who Hung On THE TREE

JESUS THE CHRIST ~ YESHUA HA YEHUDI.

Father Forgive Them For They Know Not What They Do. Luke 23:34

Into THY HANDS I COMMEND MY SPIRIT. Luke 23:46

And So It Is With Thee ~ ISRAEL ~ As You Feel Forsaken

GOD'S HEART Is "Achin" For You!! Come Back To HIM

Whatever You Do!~ COME Back As In Days Of "Yore"

When Joshua And Gideon Knew The Score~ Jehoshaphat Did Too

It Was Prayer And Praise That Brought Him Through.

ISRAEL ~ MESSIAH HE Does Not Slumber Or Sleep~ Psalm 121:4

As You Look To HIM HE Is Well Able To Keep.

HESED
Judges 6-7 & 2 Chronicles 20:1-18
Jeremiah 31:35-36 & 33:19-21 & 25-26
Isaiah 49:14-15

PASSOVER??!! "Long"

Why Can't The Jew
And The Christian
Come Together Over
THE PASSOVER??!!
The Jews Celebrate Now
What JESUS Did ~ When
In The UPPER ROOM
With HIS Friends~
Time To Pass Over,
All That Is Past ~ Has Been.
JESUS Became The Sacrifice
For All Men~ HE Even Drank
From The Cup~ The Night Before
HE Knew What Was "In Store."
Ie. "The Temple" To Be Destroyed.
In Three Days It Would Be Raised
A "Haze" To The Understanding
Of HIS Followers Then~ Later
To Be Revealed On
The Road To Emmaus When
Their Eyes Were Opened .
Then They Knew
It Was JESUS ~ YESHUA

They Were Talking To~
HE Was Alive!!!
To Digress~ The Fruit Of The
Vine Which They Drank
That Passover Night
Was A Foreshadowing
Of HIM WHOSE BLOOD
Would Be Shed ~ Slain Even Before
The Foundation Of The World.
Tho~ The World Has Hurled
And Warred Over HIM And
HIS NAME!!
A Continual Holocaust
GOD'S KORBAN
Defamed!!!!!
But Through It All
GOD HAS SHOWN MERCY
FOR HIS ULTIMATE PLAN
That The Jew And The Gentile
Might Come To Know
The SON OF MAN
JESUS THE CHRIST
YESHUA THE JEW.
Through The Unbelief
Of The Jew For A Time

GOD Has Given Space
That The Gentile Too
Might To HIM Incline.
GOD'S PASSOVER LAMB
From The "Old" To The "New."
The "Testaments" ~
And Lives ~"BORN AGAIN."
JESUS ~ YESHUA
GOD'S PASSOVER
For The Sins Of ALL Men.

HESED
Exodus 12:1 & Isaiah 53:7
John 1:29 & 36~ John 2:19-22 ~ John 3:3 & 7
Romans 11:11-36 ~ 1 Corinthians 5:7-8
Ephesians 1:4 ~

Korban~ Heb. Sacrifice

"BEHOLD THE LAMB OF GOD!"

PASSOVER~?? Will You????
This GOD Would Ask In The NAME
Of JESUS THE CHRIST ~ YESHUA THE JEW

OTHERS After PASSOVER

THE PRICE

The Holocaust
THE PRICE For
THE LAND. (ISRAEL)
What Was "Done" To
JESUS~ YESHUA
THE PRICE For The
Soul Of Man.

HESED

BUT GOD RAISED

Exiled~ Reviled~ Defiled
CRUCIFIED!
In Denial From
Those HE Came To Save!!
HE Went To The Grave~
But GOD Raised HIM Up
That With HIM
MESSIAH~ We May Sup.
Even Forevermore.
HE Said That HE
Was THE DOOR~

THE DOOR To Heaven.
GOD'S Instrument To Rid
Man Of Leaven
That Leaven In His Soul
Who Then May Become WHOLE
JESUS THE CHRIST
YESHUA THE JEW
HE Did It For You!

HESED
John 10:7 & 9 ~ Revelation 3:20 & 19:7-9

RESURRECTION !!!!

THE SECOND TIME AROUND!!

What Is The Connection Between
Passover And Yom Kippur???
Each One Needs To Pass Through
"THE D O O R" ~To Get Rid Of That
L E A V E N ~
That Would Keep Him Out Of
HEAVEN.
GOD HIMSELF Provided HIS
SCAPEGOAT -HIS KORBAN
It Was For The Sins Of All Men

A Passover Is Made By The Atoning BLOOD
Of The Passover LAMB
Provided For Us By THE GREAT I AM.
Cleansed From All Sin
BORN AGAIN ~ YOM KIPPUR
At Last~ GEULA Too~ GOD'S GIFT
Through YESHUA~JESUS THE JEW
Salvation Within ~Peace Thereby As
GOD'S REQUIREMENTS You Satisfy.
It All Started In The Land Of The Jew
And In The End
MESSIAH WILL RULE AND REIGN
From There Too
For Them HE CAME.
This Time As KING.
HIS SAINTS With
Their Crowns~
From That Heavenly
City The Second Time Around
JERUSALEM City Of PEACE
And That Among Men.
For Them HE IS Coming Back Again
Read Romans Ten ~ Nine And Eleven Too
Without Leaven - Heaven ~ Then In
The LAND OF THE JEW.

HESED
Leviticus 16:9 & 21-22 & Leviticus 17:11
John 1:29 & John 3:3 -7 & John 10:7-9
Korban ~Heb. Sacrifice & Geula~ Heb. Redemption

BECAME YOUR KORBAN
(Heb. ~ Sacrifice)

It's All About HE Who

Died For You~

Became Your Korban

The Sacrificed LAMB

The SON Of MAN.

JESUS THE CHRIST

YESHUA THE JEW~

GOD'S ATONEMENT

For You!

YOM KIPPUR

YESHUA~ Your DOOR

To Eternal Life~

Even NOW!!

As Before HIM You Bow!!!

HESED
Leviticus 17:11 ~ Isaiah 53:4-8
John 1:29 ~ John 10:9 & 27-29

YOM KIPPUR~ Heb. The Day Of Atonement

TO REPENT ~ TO CALL ~ TO ASK

"O Wretched Man That I Am."
Paul Said "This"~
Way Back "Then!!"
Job Had To Repent Before He
Could See GOD'S Prosperity
At The End Of The Book~
Called By His Name.
Take A Look.
Samuel Cried When He Didn't
Know To Whom He Must Go.
Isaiah Did Too~ "Woe Is Me!
For I Am Undone~ Because
I Am A Man Of Unclean Lips."
The Hot Coal Was Needed
To Sanctify His Tongue.
So It Is With Everyone
Who Would Come Unto HIM
Who Knows All Things.
Repentance Is Needed Unto
The CHRIST~ KING Of Kings.
JESUS THE JEW.
You Must Only ASK
To See What HE Will Do.

HESED

1 Samuel 3:4-10~Job 42:5-6 ~Isaiah 6:5-8
Jeremiah 33:3
Romans 7:22-25 ~ 1 John 3:20-21

GOD'S PATTERN

Trumpets, Pitchers, And Lanterns~
GOD'S PATTERN For Success.
I t Was Gideon Who Was Put To
The Test!!
To Man's Mind ~Could Be Folly~
Such A Combination~
 BUT~ It Was The GOD Of
ALL CREATION Who Knew
What HE Was Doing ~ When
HE Gave That Order Way Back Then
Then As Now ~HE IS THE JUDGE
Of All Men~ And So Today
Is It Not Time To Seek HIM
 For HIS WAY
A Broken Pitcher~ A Shofar Blown
A Lantern Flashing~ A Time To
Atone~ To Repent Before
The Door Will Close~ With
Destruction On The Horizon

It Is Time To Ask GOD For
HIS "Sizing" Of "The Situation.
Again~ HE IS THE GOD Of All CREATION
JESUS THE CHRIST~ YESHUA THE JEW
GOD'S GIFT To Enter In To That Which
Is New~ A NEW YEAR ~ A New Birth.
GOD Places Much Value On The Soul's Worth.

HESED
Judges 7:19-21

Confusion In The Camp Of The Enemy
GOD'S STRATEGY~Blow That Shofar
Again Today~ For That Soul To REPENT!!
To Fast And Pray~ For The Terrorist To Flee
As He Sees~ There Is One Greater Than He
The GOD Of ISRAEL HE'S Called.
Even Today~ Pray!! For This "Manifestation."
The GOD OF ALL CREATION TO ALL NATIONS.

Shofar~ A Horn~ Traditionally That Of A Ram

SUCCOT & CHRISTMAS!!!

If HE Watched Over Them
In The Wilderness Then~
Which They Now
Celebrate With Great Joy.
Could It Not Be The Same
Time When~ GOD HIMSELF
Was Born In A Manger
A Stranger~ Then
The Parallel
EMMANUEL
GOD With Us!!!
JESUS THE CHRIST
YESHUA THE JEW~
Then As Now For
HIS PEOPLE TOO!!

HESED
Deuteronomy 16:16 ~Matthew 1:23
Leviticus 17:11 ~ Isaiah 53
Ezekiel 33:1-19 ~John 3:16-17~ Romans 3:23

To Become A Son Of GOD:
RECEIVE HIM~WHOM HE Has Sent~
As The "Etrog" Is Of Great "Worth"
For Man's Soul YESHUA Was Birthed..
Of Such Great Value Is He~
GOD Has For Man A Destiny!!

SUCCOT- (Feast Of Tabernacles Or Feast Of Booths)
In The Fall...8 Days Of Festivity & Relax
Leviticus 23:33-35 & Deuteronomy 16:13-16
Zechariah 14:15-19
Etrog~ Looks Like A Lemon (Citron)~Used In Rituals At Succot.

HANUKKAH

Hanukkah - Hagigah!

A Celebration! That You Might

Become A New Creation!

HE Is The LIGHT Of The World!!

You Must Needs Know

JESUS The CHRIST

YESHUA HA YEHUDI

Eight Days Of Festivity!

May This Be A Time

For A Nativity Too

That You Might Be

BORN Anew~

GOD'S MIRACLE

Through JESUS THE JEW.

HESED

John 3:7 & 12:8 & 2 Corinthians 5:17
Hanukkah~ Heb. Dedication ~ (Commemorates The Jews' Victory
In A Battle Over The Temple In Jerusalem). Feast Of Dedication
Or Feast Of Lights~Hagigah~Heb. Celebration

CHRISTMAS TIME

Christmas Time~Time To Come In.
Have You Room In Your Inn??
The Inn Of Your Heart.
It Is In That Location
Man Gets A New Start~
Ie. In His Heart.
In The Inn There Was No Room~ Then.
But In Yours There Can Be a Nativity
For This Day Too~ The Day You Are
BORN ANEW.
Man Needs To Be If In That Last Day
With GOD He Would Be.

HESED
John 3:3 & 5 & 7 & 16 & Micah 5:2

There Was No Room For HIM Then In Bethlehem~
Micah Even Wrote That Would Be The Place ~
For The Birth Of HIS "Amazing Grace"
HIS GRACE ~ HIS PLACE- HIS GIFT ie.
JESUS THE CHRIST~ YESHUA HA YEHUDI.......
YESHUA~ Heb. JESUS & HA YEHUDI~ Heb. The Jew.

CHRISTMAS PRESENT

GOD'S PRESENT
JESUS.
Magi's Presents ~
GOD'S PRESENCE
On Earth ~ Through
HIS SON IS BIRTHED.
Now In This Time
AGAIN
In The Hearts Of Men!

HESED
Isaiah 9:6-7 & John 3:16-17

LAND OF HIS BIRTH

Land Of His Birth
But! HE Is
Multiplied!
All Over The Earth
In The Souls Of Men
Those Who Have
Been BORN AGAIN.

HESED

FOR THE NEW YEAR

GOD I Give To YOU
The "Knotted-Skein."
HE Would Say~
"Is It Not Time
You Would Allow ME
To REIGN???
Then It Is I Who Will
Take Away The Pain."

HESED

That Which Is Incongruous
That Which Would Undo Us
HE Says: "Surrender To ME."
I Am JESUS THE CHRIST
YESHUA HA YEHUDI.

HESED
As Received by Barbara Knowles
Copyright © December 31, 2009

Accounts In The Book Of ACTS
The Facts~ GOD ENACTS.... HESED

ADD~ONS

THAT STONE! !

Any "Boulder" HE Can Move!!
Even Now As Then
That Stone Was Rolled Away
From Before That Tomb.
The Size Of Which~ There
Would Not Be A "Normal"
Room Into Which It Could
"Fit!!" GOD Saw Fit To That!!
That Man Might Know HIM
Where HE Is At!!!!!!!!!!
JESUS THE CHRIST~YESHUA THE JEW
Now "B-Shemaiim"
Making Intercession For
Me And For You.

HESED
Romans 8:26

B-Shemaiim~Heb. In Heaven
(In The Heavenlies)

HOW ABOUT

How About This??
What's This?!!
Nothing New~
The Enemy's Strategy
To Block Your View
Of THE ONE Who Cares
Who Delivers From Snares
JESUS THE CHRIST
YESHUA THE JEW
PRAISE HIM! ! !
And See HIS
BREAKTHROUGH!!

HESED
Psalm 25:15~ 1 Corinthians 1:27

GOD'S BREAKTHROUGH!!
Expose The "Lies"~ Confound The Wise!!
1 Corinthians 1:27

THE CLOSED GATE!!!??

In Front Of The Closed Gate
Was A Mustard Seed Tree~
Therein Is A Parody, A Paradox
Even A Solution When You SPEAK!
As The Parable Of The Mustard Seed Tree
Therein All Is Possible~ If You Just Believe
SPEAK TO THAT MOUNTAIN!!!
Not To Grieve The SPIRIT Of THE ONE
Who Will Answer You~ JESUS THE CHRIST
YESHUA THE JEW..............
"But The Gate Is Shut!!!"~ "I Have The Key!!
All That I Ask Is That You Would Ask Of ME.
Look Unto ME~ Timing Is Involved~ Therein
Your Dilemma Is Solved.. Trust ME Too.
Then You Will See MY POWER Work For You."

HESED
Ezekiel 44:1-3 & Matthew 16:19 & 17:20
Ephesians 4:30 & 2 Timothy 1:7
Revelation 1:8 & 3:7
The Closed Gate~ The GOLDEN GATE
Through Which JESUS~ YESHUA Will
Soon Go Through ~ Jerusalem-Old City

JERUSALEM

The Wall Is Still Here~
There~ It Has Not Been
Broken Down..............
BUT~ The Tomb Is Empty
JESUS~YESHUA Is
Out Of Town...
Walls Need To Come Down.
Only Can~ Through HIM.
HE Who Broke Down That
Middle Wall Of Partition.
Partition~ Contrition Is The Key
"Come Unto ME" Said HE......
GOD'S Mercy And Pardon Then
Through JESUS The CHRIST
YESHUA THE JEW.............

HESED
Ephesians 2:14 & 1 John 1:9

"SAVLANOOT" ~ AND PEACE

"Savlanoot" And Peace~ All Are Needed
You See~ All Are Wrapped Up In
YESHUA HA YEHUDI~ HE'S Called.
"Savlanoot!!" Patience !!~
Lest You Abort GOD'S PLAN
It's All About THE SON OF MAN
JESUS THE CHRIST ~ YESHUA THE JEW
SALVATION FOR HIS CREATIONS
THEN!! Peace In The Nations.

HESED
Isaiah 9:6

Savlanoot~ Heb. Patience~
YESHUA HA YEHUDI~ Heb. JESUS THE JEW
(Who Will Answer You~)

Call Unto Me, And I Will Answer Thee, And Shew Thee
Great And Mighty Things, Which Thou Knowest Not.
JEREMIAH 33:3

GOD'S HOLY IRONY!!

From ISRAEL~ GOD'S NEW CREATION
Was Birthed...
From IRAQ ~Sin Was Birthed...
In The Garden Of Eden ie.
There It Started ~ BUT In ISRAEL
It Will End~ JESUS~ YESHUA IS
Coming Back Again~ To That LAND
And To Its People Who Have So Long
Rejected~ Been Deflected From
HIS MARVELOUS GRACE......
But GOD HIMSELF Is Creating
HIS NEW "RACE"~ Those Who
Have Run~ Begun With The SON
And Who Will End With HIM Too
JESUS THE CHRIST~
YESHUA THE JEW....
For NOW~~~~~
A Satanic War In The Heavenlies
Ie. Those Principalities~ Allowed
By The GOD Of ALL SOLEMNITIES
THE ONE Of THE BEGINNING
THE ONE OF THE END
THE ALPHA AND OMEGA IS
COMING BACK AGAIN!!!!!!!!

From IRAQ To ISRAEL~
GOD'S HOLY IRONY
Displayed For The World To See
JESUS THE CHRIST~
YESHUA HA YEHUDI......

HESED
Isaiah 33:20-24
Ephesians 6:11-18
Romans Chapters 9-10-11
Revelation 1:8
As Received by Barbara Knowles
Copyright © July 23, 2006

Note~ Not By The "Works"
We Have "Done" BUT By
"THE FINISHED WORK" Of
GOD'S ONLY SON~ YESHUA ie.
JESUS THE CHRIST~YESHUA
HA YEHUDI.. Ephesians 2:8-9

YESHUA HA YEHUDI-Heb. JESUS THE JEW

Re. Zion~ "The People That Dwell Therein
Shall Be Forgiven..." Isaiah 33:24

IRAQ~ ISRAEL & YOU!!!!

IRAQ Was Where The Problem
Got Started~ Later For ISRAEL
The Red Sea HE Parted,...........
Now HE Is Ready To Do It Again
To Enable Man To Part With
His Sin...........
For ISRAEL HE IS COMING
Back Too..For Thirty Three Years
HE Was Already THERE!!!
Since Then Other Souls By
HIS SPIRIT Was Sent To Repair.
IRAQ...........BUT
To ISRAEL HE WILL RETURN
Most Important~ HIS LOVE
Not To Spurn~ JESUS THE CHRIST
YESHUA THE JEW~
GOD'S SOLUTION For The Pollution
In The Souls Of Men~ HE Who Said
"Ye Must Be BORN AGAIN
To Nicodemus Then~ The Jew
Who Asked How???? At Eighty
Years Old It Was THE MESSIAH
Who Told HIM ~ How....

Now In Sin You Have
Been~ But NOW! BOW!!
For This HE Has Long Waited
That To Sin You Would
Not "Cow-Tow."
To HIM It Is Not Too Late
HE Only Gives And Has The
POWER To Reverse Your "Fate."
HOLINESS Or HELL!!
Come To THE WELL Of
HIS SALVATION ie. THEN
From Sin And Its Penalty
HE WILL SET YOU FREE!!!!

HESED
Isaiah Chapter 12 ~John 1:12
John 3:& 5 & 7

Mesopotamia ~Then~ Now The
Battleground For The Souls Of Men.
Sin The Denominator~ The Dominator
Until~ Man Of This Has Had His "Fill!!"

THE COMING

The Coming Of THE LORD
Draweth Nigh.
We That Are HIS
Need To Testify!!!
Verify That Which HE
Has Done For Us Personally
All By Way Of
JESUS THE CHRIST
YESHUA HA YEHUDI.

HESED

COMING IN

Coming In To "THE REST"
As You Partake Of "HIS LIKENESS"~
CHRIST Formed In You..........ie.
Therein Is Your Hope For Glory..

HESED
Hebrews 4 & Colossians 1:27
As Received by Barbara Knowles
Yom Kippur October 9, 2008

YESHUA BIFNEEM

YESHUA BIFNEEM
LO LAYEETEEM!!
COL HA ZMAN.
YESHUA~ WHO ADON!!

HESED

JESUS INSIDE

JESUS ON THE INSIDE!!
NOT SOMETIMES!!
ALL THE TIME.
JESUS~ HE IS LORD!

Hebrews 13:5
.... For HE Hath Said I Will
Never Leave Thee Nor Forsake Thee.